A Newfoundland ALPHABET

Words and Pictures by
Dawn Baker

For Samantha

Note to kids:

The illustrations for this book were created with simple and inexpensive art supplies. These consist of regular pencils, coloured pencils, charcoal pencils, and chaulk pastels. The paper used was textured drawing paper. Why don't you pull out some of your art supplies and complete a drawing of some of the things in your life?

You'll find that beauty is all around you, when you take the time to really look.

Library and Archives Canada Cataloguing in Publication

Baker, Dawn, 1962-
    A Newfoundland alphabet / words and pictures by Dawn Baker.

ISBN 978-1-897317-90-7

    1. English language--Alphabet--Juvenile literature. 2. Alphabet books. 3. Newfoundland and Labrador--Pictorial works--Juvenile literature. 4. Newfoundland and Labrador--Social life and customs--Juvenile literature. I. Title.

PE1155.B337 2010   j421'.1   C2010-905377-X

PRINTED IN CANADA

Pennywell Books is an imprint of Flanker Press Limited.

FLANKER PRESS
P.O. BOX 2522, STATION C
ST. JOHN'S, NL A1C 6K1 CANADA
TOLL-FREE: 1-866-739-4420
WWW.FLANKERPRESS.COM

15 14 13 12 11 10   1 2 3 4 5 6 7 8 9

We acknowledge the financial support of: the Government of Canada through the Book Publishing Industry Development Program (BPIDP); the Canada Council for the Arts which last year invested $20.1 million in writing and publishing throughout Canada; the Government of Newfoundland and Labrador, Department of Tourism, Culture and Recreation.

A Antlers

B Beaches, Barrens, Bakeapples

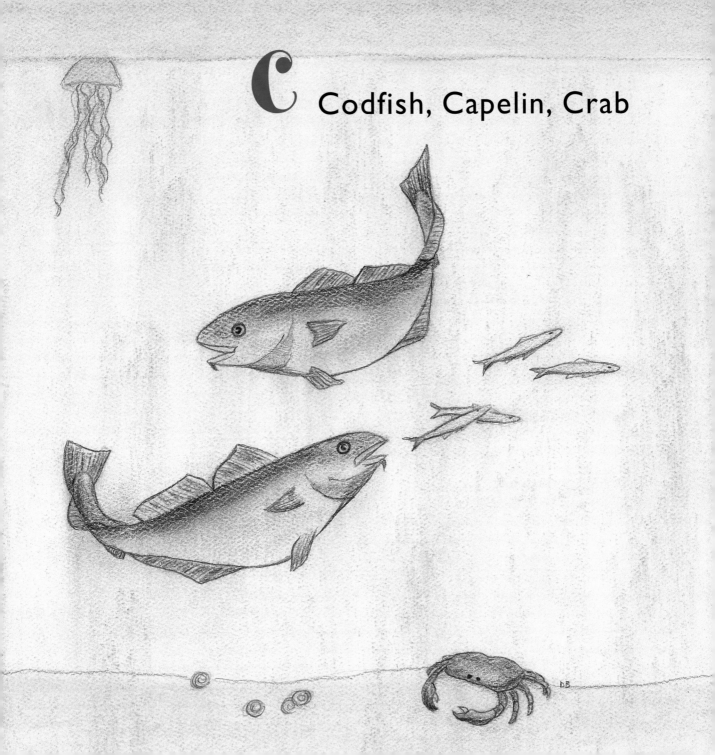

C

Codfish, Capelin, Crab

D Digging for clams

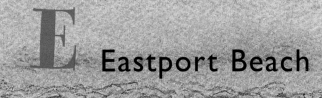

E Eastport Beach

F

Ferry, Fog

G Gull, Gannet, Grebe, Grouse

H   Hard Tack

I Iceberg

J

Jam Jams

K Komatik

L Lobster

M Mummers

N Newfoundland Pony, Newfoundland Dog

O Outport

P Puffin

Q Quilt, Quiet

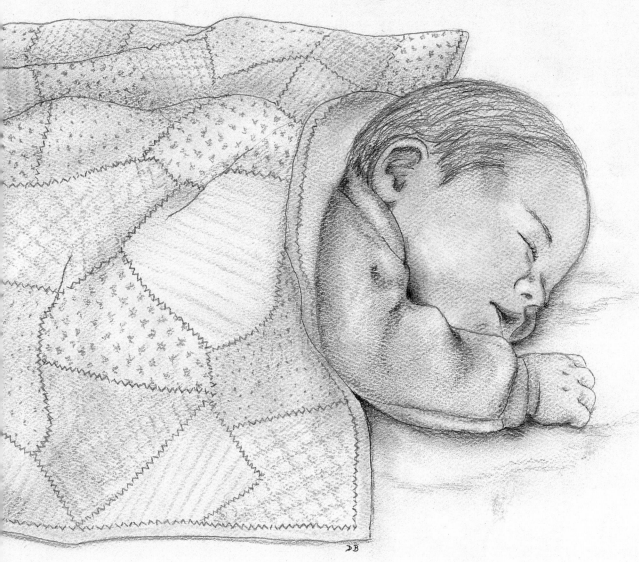

R River

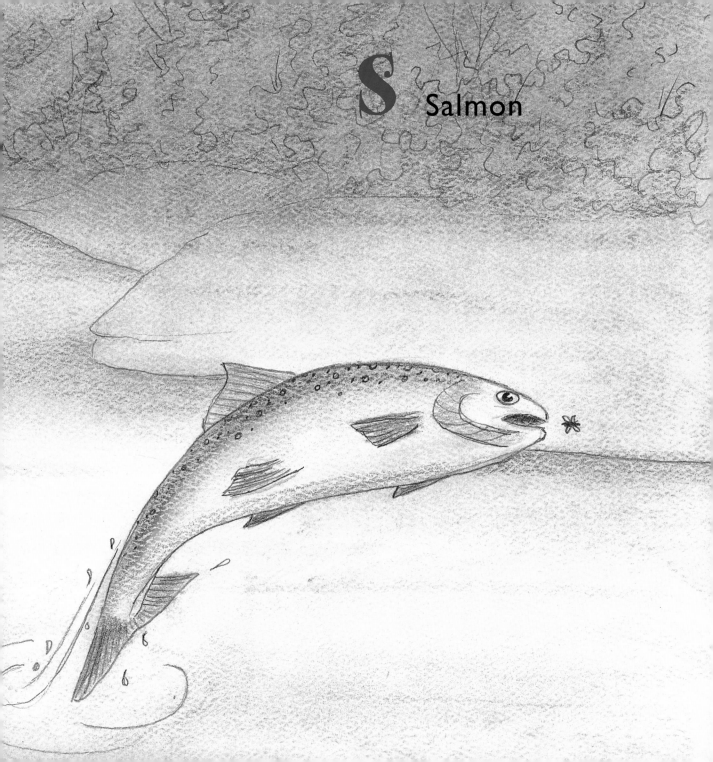

S Salmon

T Toutons, Tea

U Urchins from the sea

V Vista from the cape

W Waves, Whales

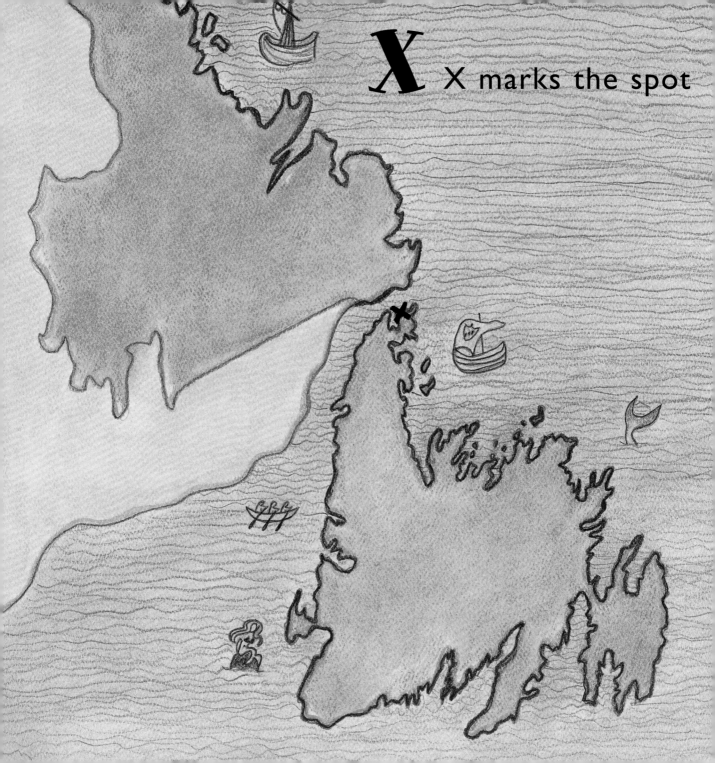

X X marks the spot

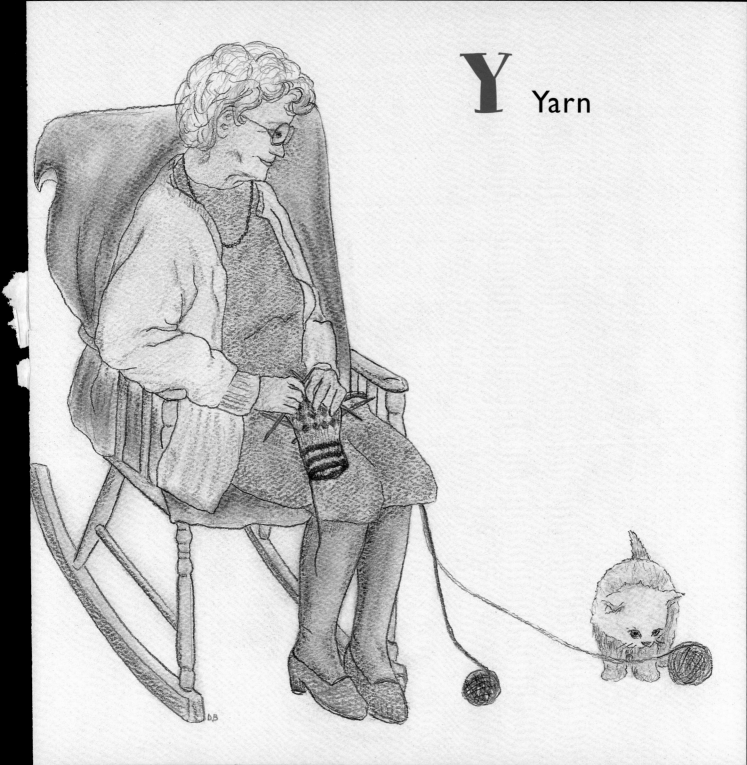

Y Yarn

Z Zest for life